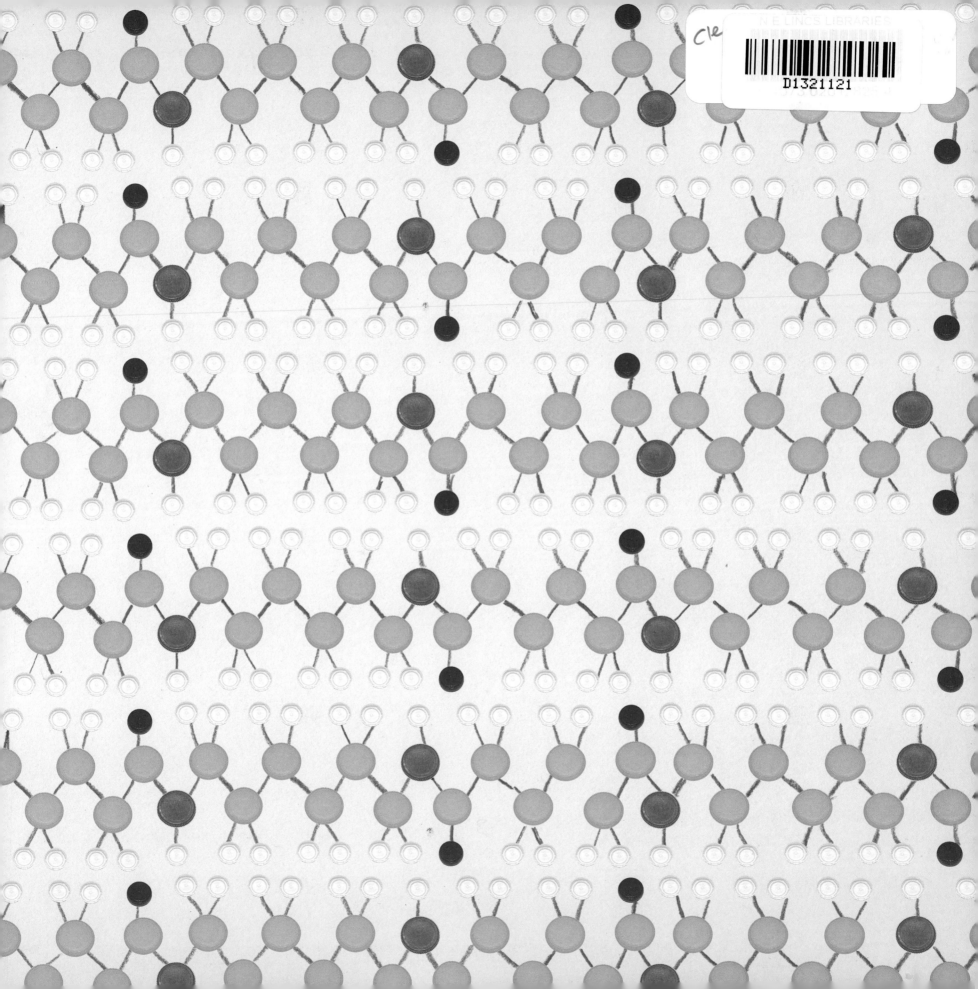
N E LINCS LIBRARIES

Cle

D1321121

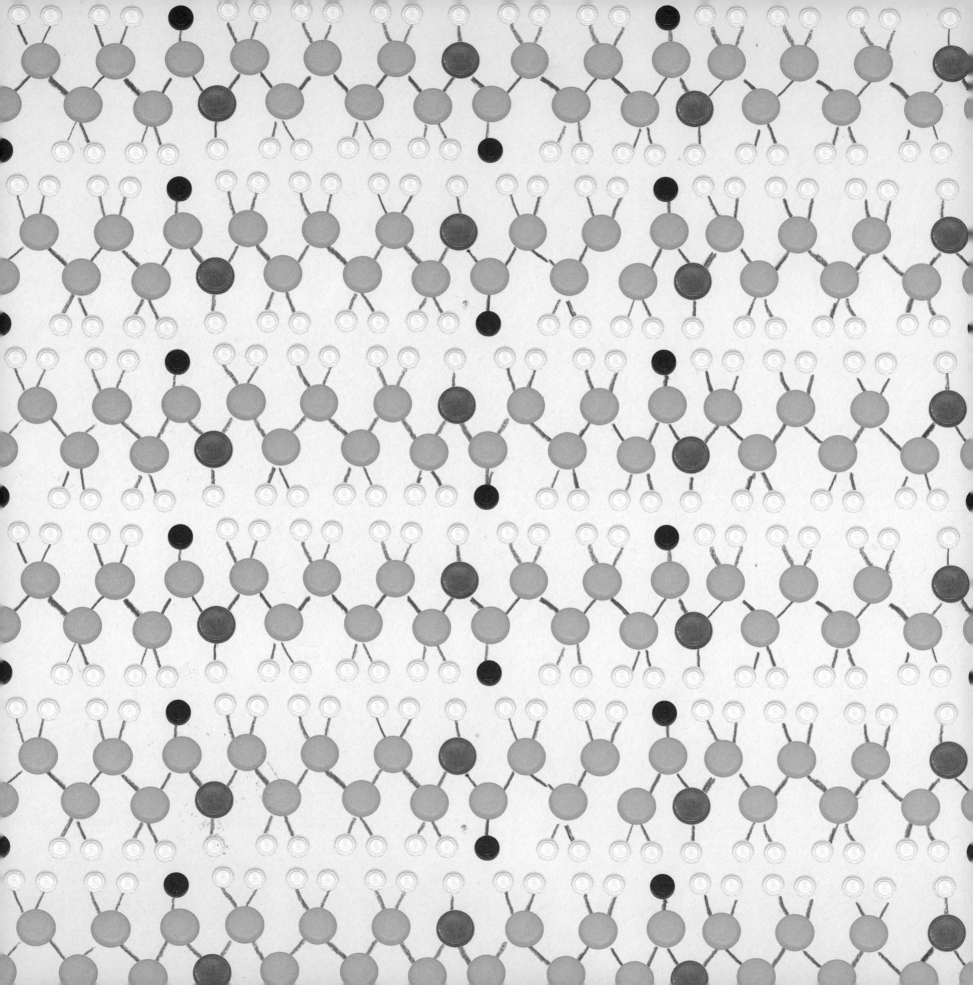

A PLANET FULL OF PLASTIC

by Neal Layton

wren
&rook

NORTH EAST LINCOLNSHIRE LIBRARIES
WITHDRAWN FROM STOCK
AUTHORISED:

Hello you!

Who, me?

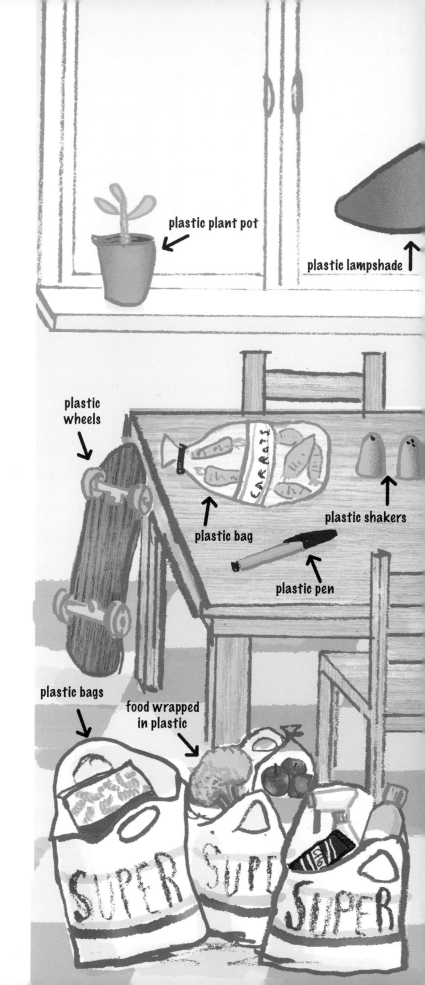

plastic plant pot

plastic lampshade

plastic wheels

plastic bag

plastic shakers

plastic pen

plastic bags

food wrapped in plastic

That's right. Quick question: do you ever think about what things are made of?

Because some things are made of paper, like this book. Some things are made of wood. Or metal. Or glass.

But some things, in fact lots of things,
are made of something called PLASTIC.

plastic clock

plastic lid

plastic tub

microfibre cloth

plastic bottle

plastic basket

plastic squeezy bottle

plastic label

plastic milk carton

plastic packet

plastic lid

plastic buttons

plastic handle

plastic toy

nylon lead

MILK

TOMATO SAUCE

Isn't plastic **FANTASTIC!** It comes in lots of different shapes, sizes and colours.

Sometimes
it's bendy,

sometimes
it's hard.

Sometimes
it's big,

and sometimes
it's really really tiny.

If you look around you, plastic is EVERYWHERE.

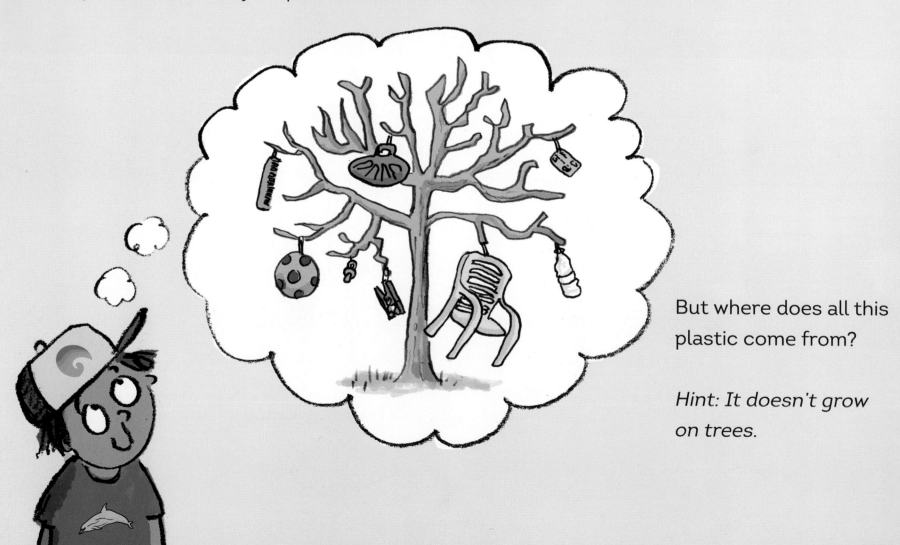

But where does all this
plastic come from?

*Hint: It doesn't grow
on trees.*

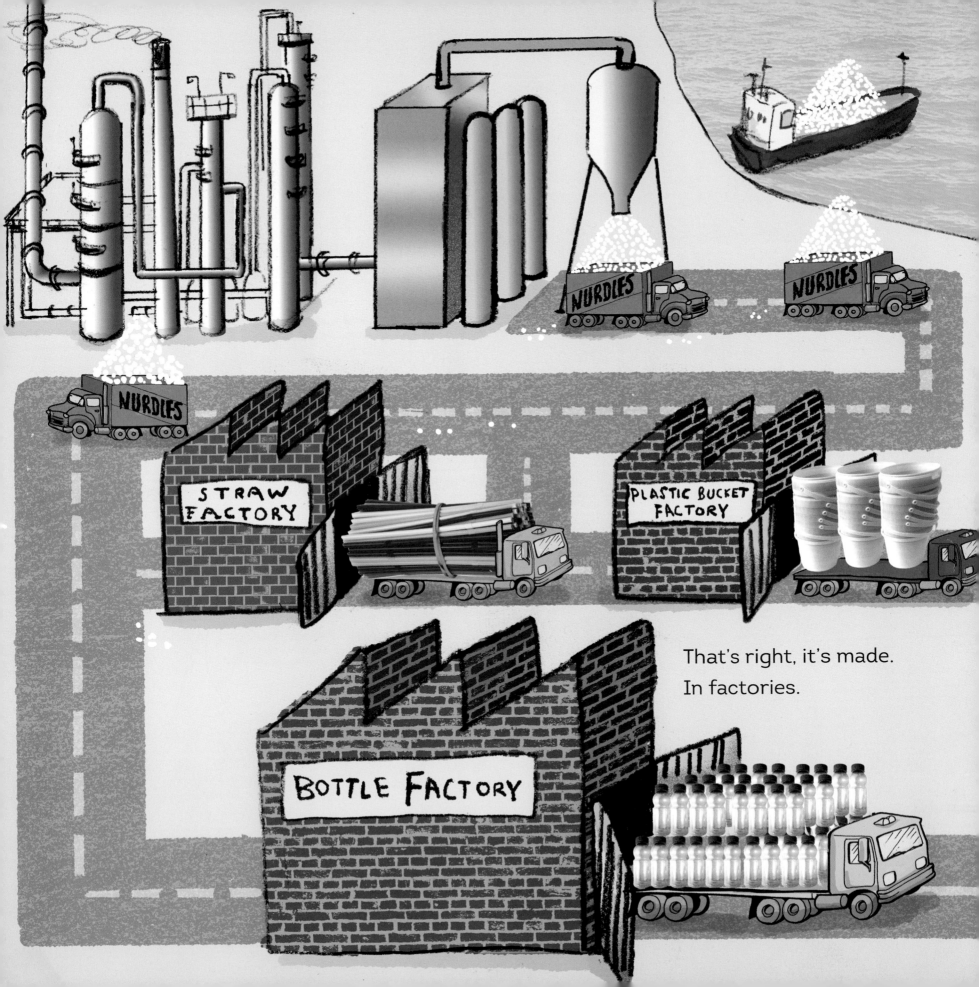

That's right, it's made.
In factories.

You see, 150 years ago there wasn't any plastic. Only materials like wood, metal, paper and stone.

And then one day, super-chemist Mr Baekeland made an incredible discovery...

CRAZY! Groovy!

"**Plastic is FANTASTIC!**" they all said.

nylon flag

plastic straw

plastic glasses

plastic food box

plastic-coated cup

plastic carrier bag

plastic chair

nylon lounge suit

nylon stockings

plastic space suit

unbreakable plastic plate

plastic drink bottle

They started making lots of it. And using it for just about everything they could.

plastic computer

Welcome to the future...

plastic nails

mostly plastic plane

Lycra sportswear

plastic boots

nylon flares

plastic flip-flops

plastic trainers

But there was a problem.

If you look around, you won't just see plastic where it's meant to be.

You'll also see it where it's NOT meant to be. Because one of the most amazing things about plastic is that it doesn't

biodegrade

like natural things.

Oof, that's a big word. What does it mean?

plastic bottle

Let me explain...

If a leaf drops to the ground, it will go yellow, then brown, and all skinny and thin, until it's just mud and dust.

It takes a few months. You can't see them, but bugs are eating the leaf, breaking it down.

And it's the same with an apple core or any natural thing. This is called biodegrading.

APPLE CORES TAKE ABOUT EIGHT WEEKS TO BIODEGRADE

After one month

After about one week

CLOSE-UP OF WHAT IS HAPPENING

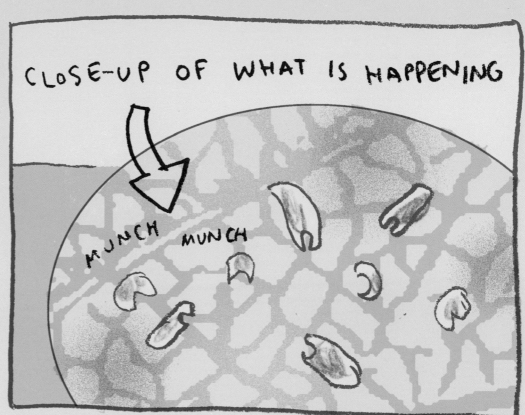

MUNCH   MUNCH

After about six months

MUD AND DUST

How long things take to BIODEGRADE

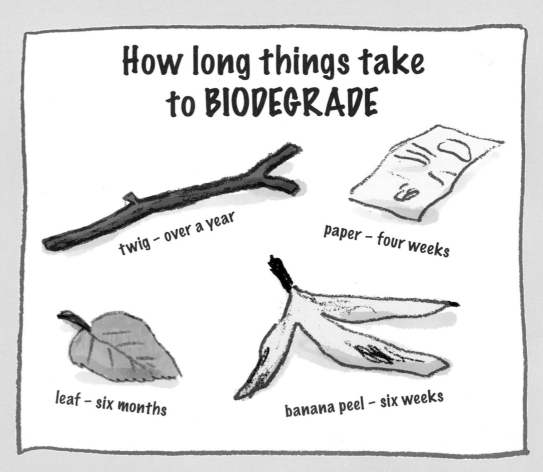

twig – over a year

paper – four weeks

leaf – six months

banana peel – six weeks

plastic bottle

After six months

After one year

After one month

Many years later

Plastic is different. If it drops to the ground, it just stays there.

For years.

And years.

And years.

It doesn't biodegrade.

REALLY?

Yes, really.

This makes plastic super-useful, because it lasts a long time.

But it also creates a problem.

If plastic ends up where it's not meant to be, it will stay there for years and years. Until eventually the weather breaks it down into smaller and smaller pieces. Of plastic.

A huge amount of this plastic eventually ends up in the ocean.

from toilets

MEGA MESS CORP.

from plastic factories

Some of it floats to the top of the ocean and stays there.

And some of it sinks to the bottom of the ocean and stays there.

All of this is a really big problem for animals.

Some of them get tied up in it.

Some of them try
to eat the plastic.

Because of circular currents in the oceans, the bits of plastic have
collected together, creating five enormous garbage patches full of plastic.

The most famous is called the North Pacific Garbage Patch.
It is currently THREE TIMES the size of France.

Most of the plastic in these patches has broken up into pieces that are so small you can hardly see them. A microplastic is any piece smaller than this

These are even more of a problem than big bits. Animals think they are food, so they eat them. The microplastics fill up their tummies, leaving no room for proper food.

And the plastics often carry and contain nasty toxins, so if a small fish eats them, it can be poisoned. And so might a bigger fish that eats the small fish for dinner. And then all the way up the food chain!

Some scientists think there will soon be more plastic than fish in the sea.

But I don't want animals
to get hurt! And I don't want
our planet to fill up with plastic.

Well, we all need to try to reduce how much plastic we use every day. The less we use, the less we have to clean up!

And people who make stuff for us need to think carefully about what they do with plastic. Creating things that will be thrown away in minutes, but stay in the environment for ever, isn't right.

People make nearly 330 million tonnes of plastic each year. Around half of it is only used once and then thrown away.

Reduce

Lots of plastic things are meant to be reused over and over again.
Let's make sure we do!

And if we have finished using a plastic thing, perhaps we can pass it
to someone else.

When the plastic stuff has been reused lots of times, it should be recycled so it can be turned into new plastic things, not just thrown away.

But plastic can only be recycled a few times before it stops being useful, and not all plastic can be recycled.

So environmentalists are teaching people about the problem, because everyone needs to help fix it.

Scientists are coming up with clever ideas too, experimenting with special bugs which might help plastics biodegrade, and finding new materials for us to use.

PERHAPS A

A SOLAR-POWERED WHEEL TO COLLECT PLASTIC

It'll take each and every person working together
to stop the planet filling up with plastic.

It's a big job, but I reckon we can do it.

Thanks for listening.

How you can help

There are loads of ways to help solve the plastic problem! You could...

1 Get creative and reuse the plastic you already own!

bottle to water plants

plastic bottle as a mini greenhouse

shaker made from tub

pen pot made from tub

plastic trays make great paint palettes

2 Ask your family to replace anything made from or packaged in plastic with more eco-friendly options.

3 Grab some gloves and take part in a clean-up near you – whether it's on a beach, in a park or on the street. You could do it for 2 minutes or 20!

Ask a grown-up to visit http://beachclean.net for some tips!

And you know, it's not just grown-ups who have BIG ideas...

HANNAH TESTA knew that more people needed to learn about the plastic problem. By the time she was 14, she had created Plastic Pollution Awareness Day!

BOYAN SLAT was just 16 when he realised how much plastic filled our oceans. Since then, he's invented a system called Ocean Cleanup, which gathers up plastic to be recycled.

MELATI AND ISABEL WIJSEN started campaigning against plastic bags in their home country of Indonesia when they were aged 10 and 12. Their campaign, Bye Bye Plastic Bags, has gone global.

Researching and writing this book changed my life. My hope is that reading it might change yours too. So, can you think of a big idea to help save the planet?

MY BIG IDEA

?

GLOSSARY

Bakelite	The first human-made plastic, named after Leo Baekeland.
Microplastic	Small, barely visible pieces of plastic that pollute the environment.
Nylon	A type of plastic often used for making clothes, rope and brush bristles.

Huge thanks to David Jones of Just One Ocean/University of Portsmouth,
without whose help this book would not have been possible.
And also to Clare Seek for being an inspiration to all around her.

First published in Great Britain in 2019 by Wren & Rook

Copyright © Neal Layton, 2019

All rights reserved.

HB ISBN: 978 1 5263 6173 8
PB ISBN: 978 1 5263 6176 9
E-book ISBN: 978 1 5263 6177 6
10 9 8 7 6 5 4 3 2 1

Wren & Rook
An imprint of Hachette Children's Group
Part of Hodder & Stoughton
Carmelite House, 50 Victoria Embankment, London EC4Y 0DZ

An Hachette UK Company
www.hachette.co.uk
www.hachettechildrens.co.uk

Publishing Director: Debbie Foy
Senior Editor: Liza Miller
Creative Director: Sophie Stericker

Printed in China

Picture acknowledgements: The publisher would like to thank the following for permission
to reproduce their pictures: Front cover lamnao / Shutterstock.com;
pp. 15, 16–17, 20–21, 22–23, 25 © David Jones.

No part of this publication may be reproduced, stored in a retrieval system, or transmitted, in any form
or by any means, without the prior permission in writing of the publisher, nor be otherwise circulated
in any form of binding or cover other than that in which it is published and without a similar condition
including this condition being imposed on the subsequent purchaser.

Every effort has been made to clear copyright. Should there be any inadvertent omission,
please apply to the publisher for rectification.

The website addresses (URLs) included in this book were valid at the time of going to press. However, it is
possible that contents or addresses may have changed since the publication of this book. No responsibility
for any such changes can be accepted by either the author or the publisher.

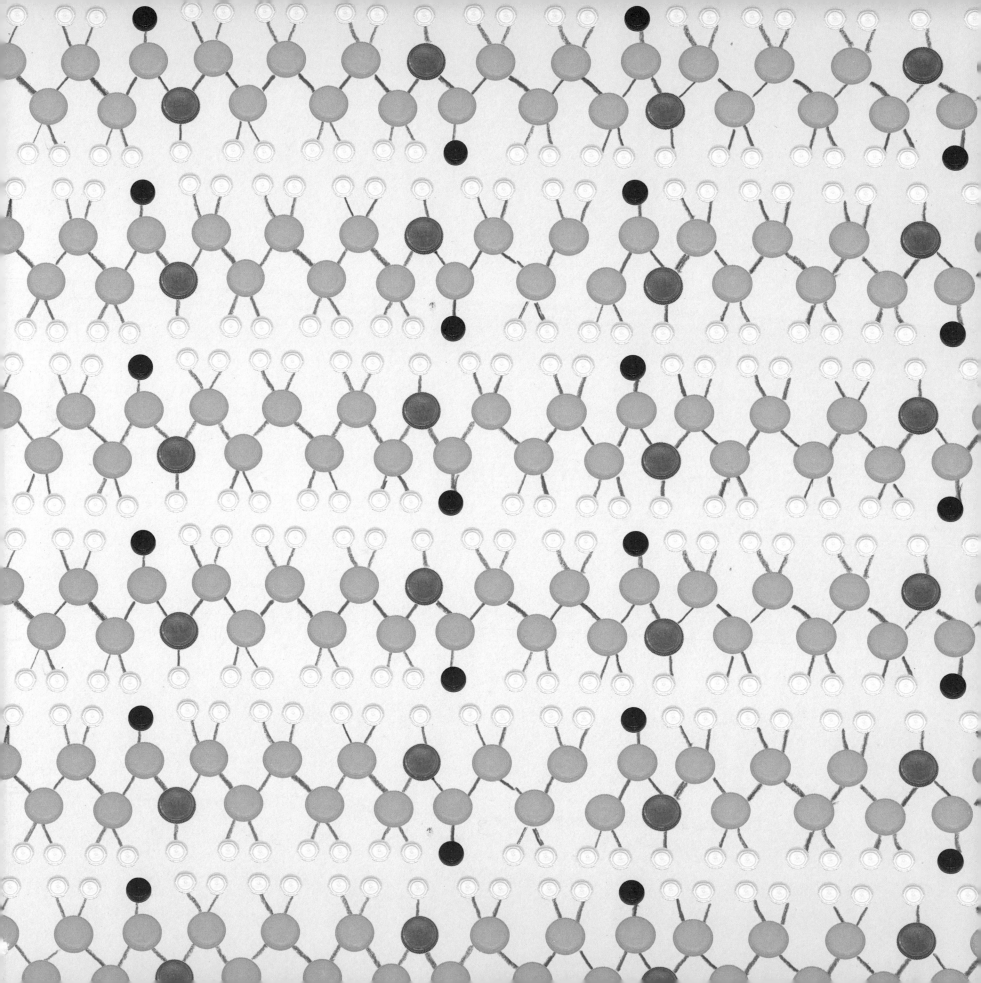

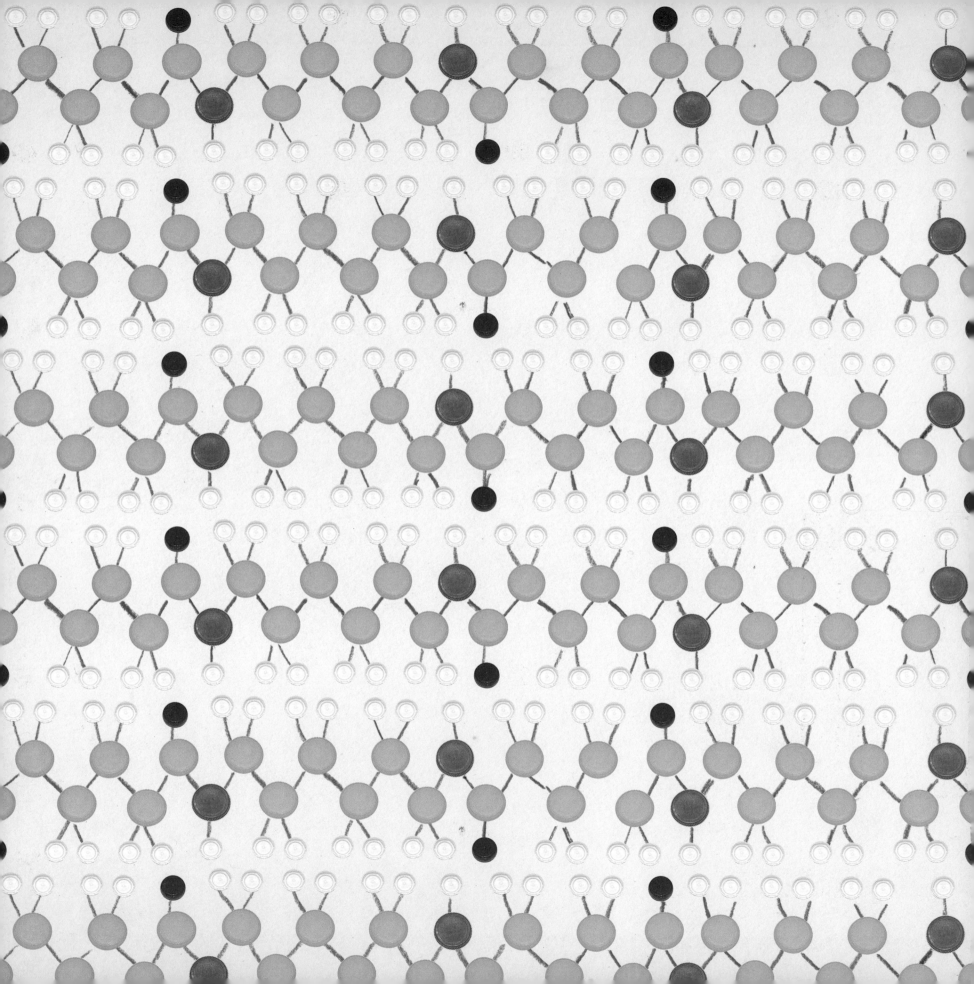